CALLIGRAFFITI

CALLIGRAFFITI
CALLIGRAFFITI

CALLIGRAFFITI
CALLIGRAFFITI
CALLIGRAFFITI

LACHLAN J McDOUGALL

©2024

Lachlan J McDougall

ISBN: 9798377758181

All rights reserved. No part of this book may be reproduced without express written permission of the author.

Ipswich, Queensland, Australia

lachlan.mcdougall@gmail.com

lachlanjmcdougall.wordpress.com

or find the Author on Facebook (Lachlan J McDougall – Author), Instagram (@lachlanjmcdougall) and Twitter (@AuthorLachlan)

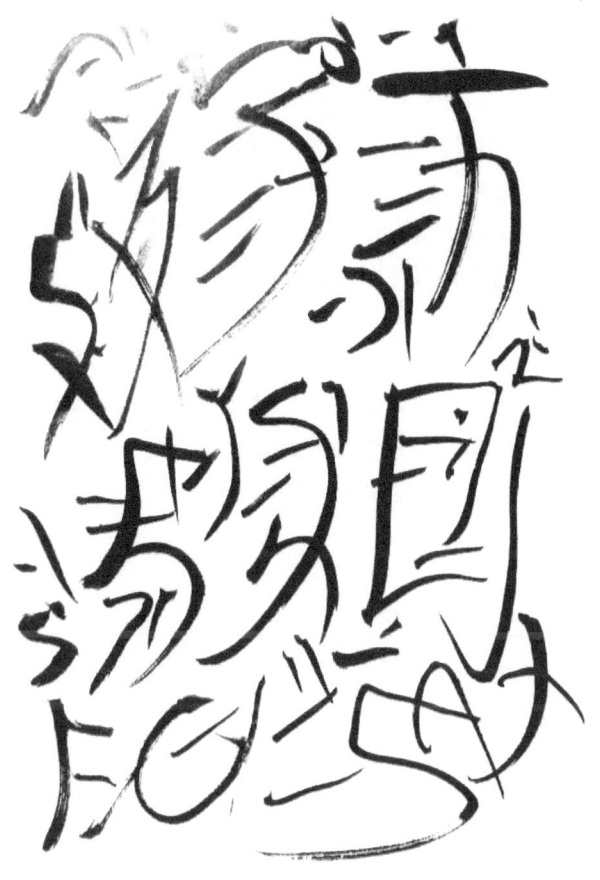

This book originally appeared in mid 2022 as a free hand-printed zine sent out to the author's mailing network. Some copies of the book are probably still circulating.

It has been gathered here into this book in the interests of posterity. A proper bound book to keep together all the wild ephemera that stalks the earth.

If you want to get your hands on a copy of the original zine, try emailing the author at lachlan.mcdougall@gmail.com

You never know your luck!

Bread, milk
Cheese, dignity
I changed the oil
Just last winter

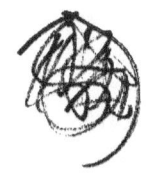

        Ice on the pavement
        Buffalo wings, ranch
        Animal rights, satori
        I have made a list of
          The things I require

Gas for the oven
A Christmas turkey
Gobble gobble
Fat cat spread
The presents this year
Are warbling thin
Bread, milk

Dignity

A dying breed

Of vanity

                              The cats

                              Are mewling

                              Calico Jane

                              Bread, milk

                              Animal rights

                              We're looking after

                              Our own

                              Car

                              Won't start

                              I changed the oil

                              Just last

                              Winter

The streets are frosted

Over—chains

On the tires, I

Have made a list of

Nothing

And

Everything

All the things

I require

Before

I retire

Into the orange nowhere

                  Om mani padme hum

                  We have reached a level

                        Living in

                  The moment of suffering

                  Buffalo wings, carbonara

                    Frozen meals built

                        For one

                  Om mani padme hum

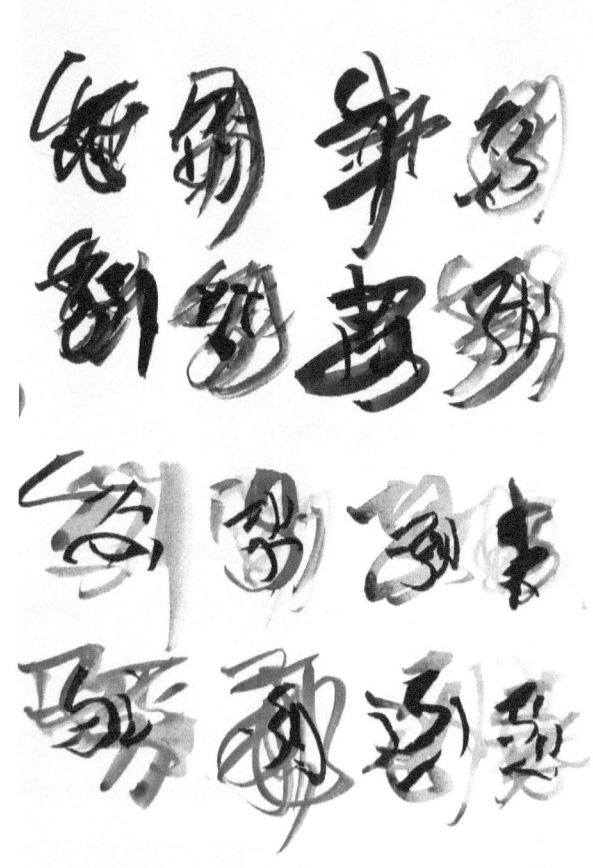

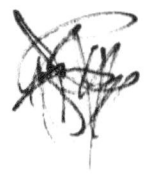

One shot

from

a loaded gun.

I saw time

pass through

the barrel

of

the bible.

"We're just a glob of grease

and we're on our way

down..."

(Brion at Bedtime)

"never mind all that my dear

never mind the bright salutation

...

never mind the fires of hell"

—if we play our cards right,

we won't have to look—

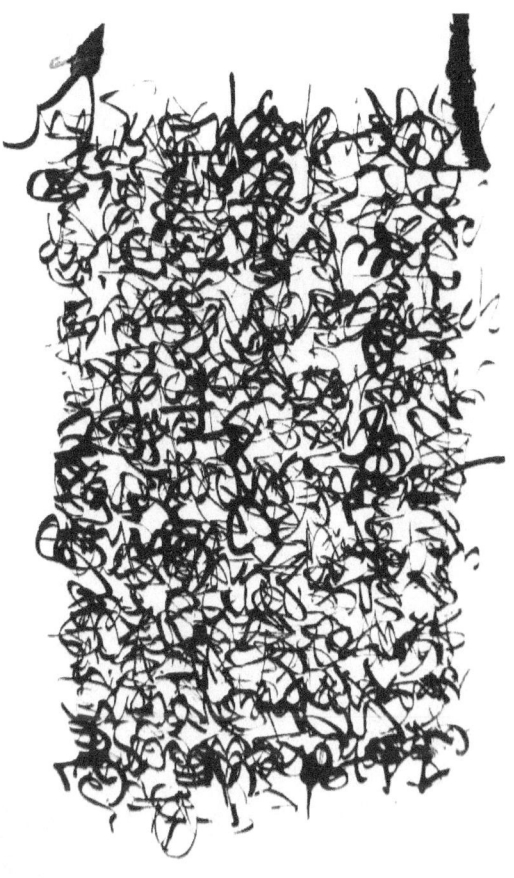

I paint a picture

                                      It's not sacred

Take a picture

                Develop

                Reproduce

                Indefinitely

I paint a picture

                                    with my words

I paint a picture

                                    of my word

My word

                                      is a painting

                Take a picture

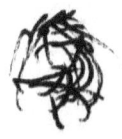

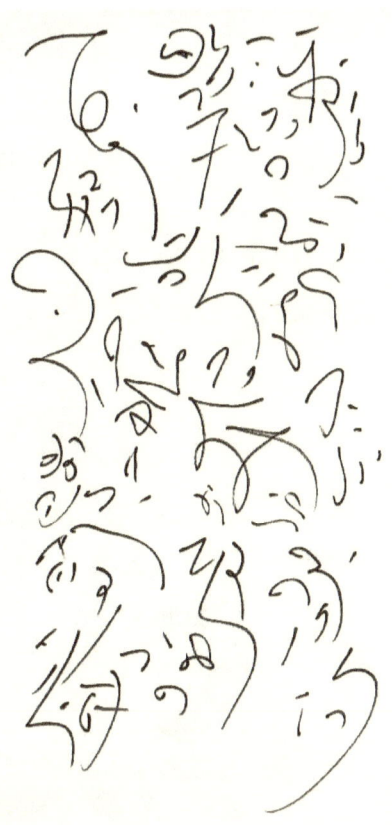

Take a picture

                                        A picture take

Take a tincture

                                        A tincture make

                We're all on board

Have you tried writing

                                          It down

              ???

You'd be surprised

When the words

                Run

                                        Away

With you

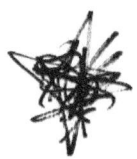

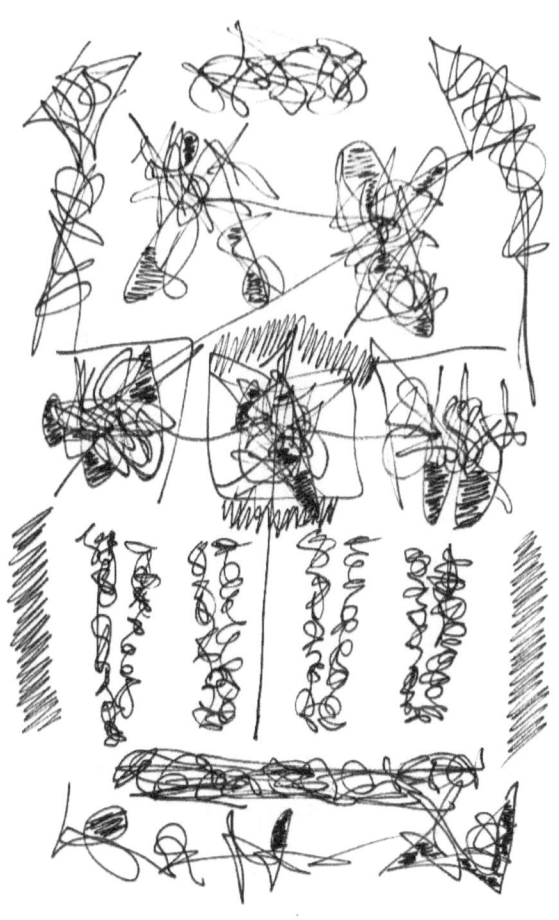

Calligraffiti

    The word is a Vandal

    Even the act of writing

                      is a crime

    Your words no longer

      Make sense

                      Or don't

    We extend into

    The Sunset of Fire

Calligraffiti

      Synchronise your brush

      With the cosmic

                      Antenna

    What do you really have to say?

      Make your crime

      Like a burglary

          Words are not sacred!

      Take them

Any time you want

Calligraffiti

    The word is

    Of course,

                  A Crime

    The fire-pen saw to that

        With one stroke

        You were behind

        The iron curtain

        Of words—jailor

        Coming through

                "Yes officer, it won't

                    Happen again"

Calligraffiti

    What is your true name?

    The one your parents

    Didn't give you?

            The one you

            Never knew?

    What is the movement

    Of the brush

    When the pictures are talking?

    What does your name have to say?

Calligraffiti

        The Word is a Picture

        Take a picture

        Take a word

        Take it any time

        Shuffle it up

                Like Alphabet Soup

        Your brush like

                A machine gun

        Your brush like

        Atom Bomb

Calligraffiti

    The Phoenix Word

    The Mountain Word

    The Word of Assassins

               Hashashin

                Hash is In

    The Garden of Delight

    Just where is it taking you?

    Can you write it down?

            Can you take a picture?

Calligraffiti

    The words are your weapon

Calligraffiti

    The words will drag you down

Calligraffiti

    Kicking and screaming

Calligraffiti

    The sunset dusk orange glow

Calligraffiti

    Paint your words just don't

    Let your words paint you

               Into a corner

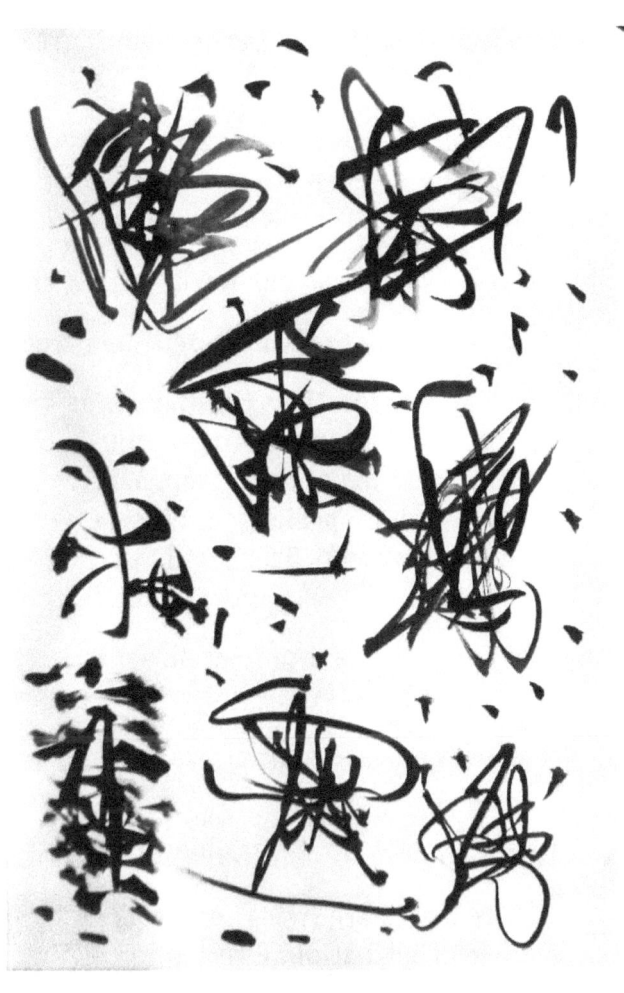

Reading is an act of creation! Writing is an act of destruction! Set the words free!

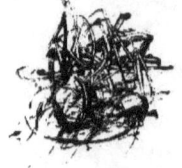

Who are you?

Where are you?

What are you doing?

Are your words your own?

Destroy the words! Set them free!

Fingerpaint the sky—the words are there—buffalo, china, fingerprint—fold them back, make them stop. When you speak a word, it speaks you. Write a word and it is written. The past is written— unwrite the future!

Mektoub—it is written—well, set it free!

This is the space age and we are here to go.

This is the age of undifferentiated living.

The words are living for us like a bad movie. Tell that old director to call cut! Now there's an idea, why don't we get a little party together? Hang the paintings! Hang the words! Hang the captains of industry! Use your brush like Atom Bomb—blast that word into frozen space. Use your brush like psychic hygiene—rub that word out! Writing is an act of destruction—set the words free!

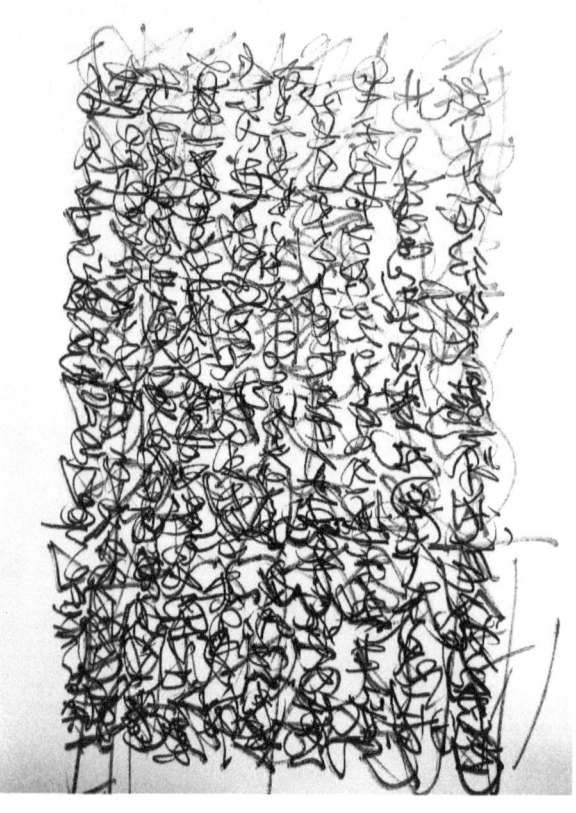

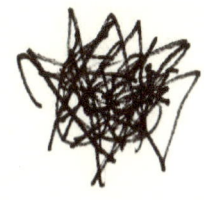

A Book is a River

A Book is a Giver

        A River is a Book

        A Liver is a Look

A Giver is a Liver

    Is a River is Aquiver

    By Hook By Crook

    By Liver By Book

A River a Book a Pot of Patchouli

    A Giver a Look a Patch of Pot Truly

Get that Stink Out

Get that Drink Out

        Get out that Sink

        Get in the Pink

Sink in the Stink

Or Get Out of the Think

    We Wink a Drink in Calligraphy Ink

    Sink in the Stink of Ink, I Think

Live Wire, Highwire

Car Tyre, House Fire

A River A Book

By Hook or By Crook

        Get Out of the Think

        Get Out of the Ink

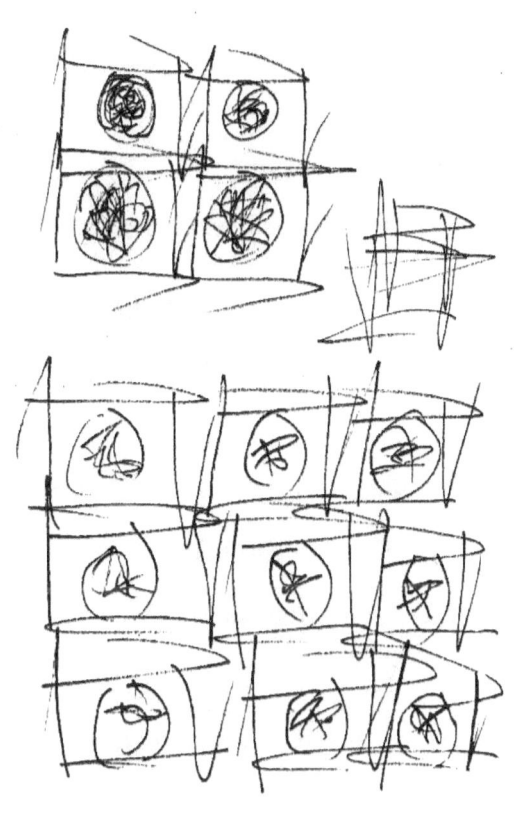

Wonderful World Wonderful Life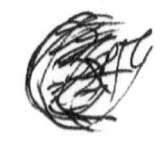
Wonderful Girl Wonderful Wife
Wonderful Wonderful Wonderful
Wonder I Wonder
What Lies Under?

        Underful World Underful Life
                Under I'm Under
            What Lies Asunder?

    Thunder the Girl Thunder the Wife
        Thunder and Plunder
          Pallet and Strife

Wonderful World Wonderful Life
Thunder and Lightning
        Pallet and Strife

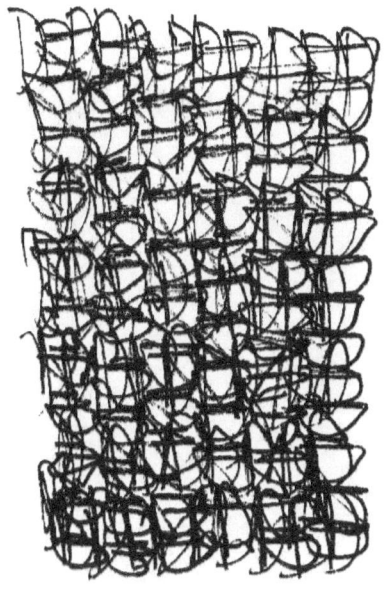

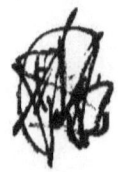

You're into Calligraphy?

I'm into destruction.

But you talk of using your brush as a weapon.

The typewriter does it better.

Then why calligraphy?

The typewriter can't paint a picture—
there we differ.

You paint your words?

A painting is a picture, a word is anything but. I turn the word into the thing itself. Wind back the tape—there's nothing left but the recording.

You think language takes on a different aspect?

There is a planet not too far from here where they speak in the picture language. Every word a perfect work of art. Communication is impossible, but boy is it beautiful.

And this would improve things?

Communication is already impossible on our so-called Earth—our neighbours are simply honest about it.

Do you think the written word could be returned to communication?

I think we've come too far. Why speak at all? The script is already written.

So why poetry then?

A poem is simply a way of saying nothing all dressed up in garlands. Who told the poets they could think? Let's just doll this up and let the reader do the work.

You don't think you're saying anything with your work?

Nothing left to say. *Mektoub*—it is written.

What advice do you have for the next generation of writers?

There's nothing to it! You get what you pay for.

Do you think there's hope for writing in the future?

I think there's guerrillas in the wings. They're not writing, they're fomenting.

You see a revolution?

A work of art is from a different time—it does not move. Writing is in movement. When you paint your picture, see that it moves.

But about the future of writing—are you saying the written word is a dead end?

Our friends on Planet X have done away with novels and poetry, and a dreary old time it is. The trick with pictures, nothing moves. Our artists are working on the timestream, I see a new future, a new past. I see a novel that can't be pinned down, poetry that shifts with the wind.

And the script?

Oh just call *cut!* Let's do a re-write job!

So there is hope after all?

Planet X is coming home to roost—there is little time. Throw out your novels, tear up your poetry—let's get busy on a moving picture!

And what advice do you have for these future artists?

Sounds like that machine is almost out of tape—better change the materials...

(The tape cuts off here—nothing further remains.)

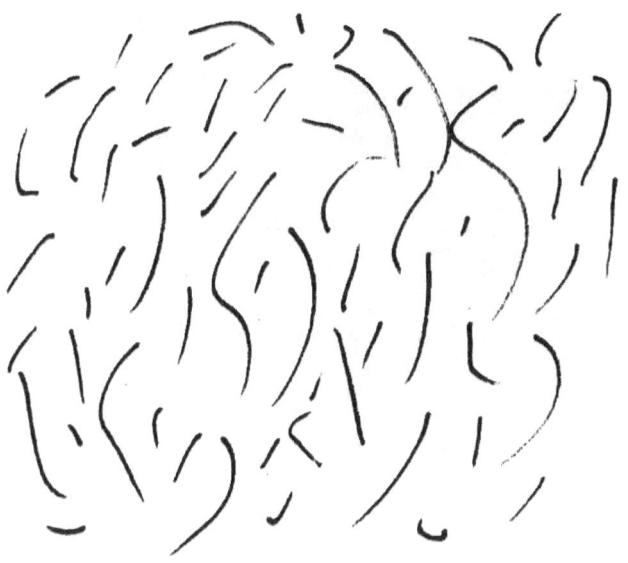

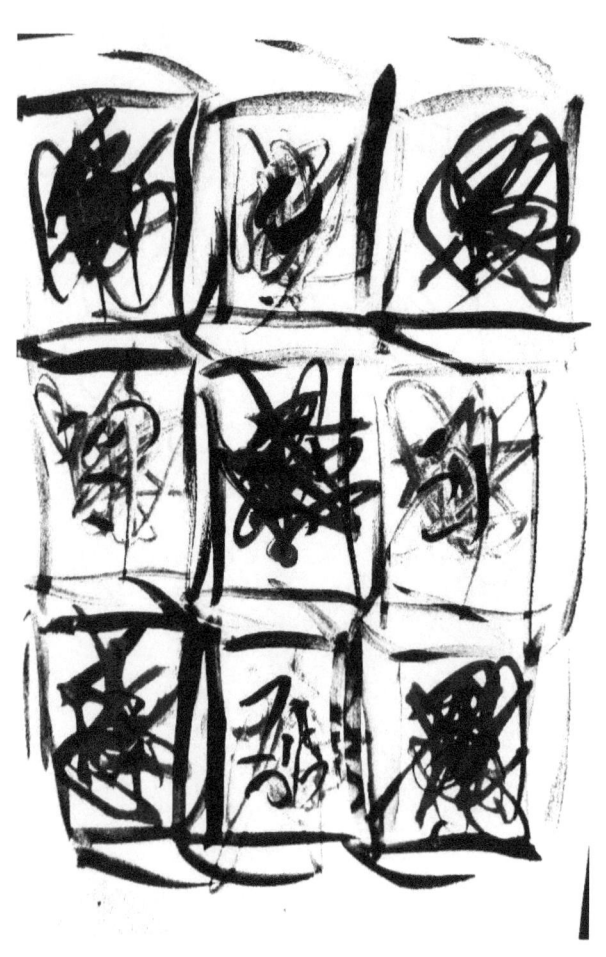

www.ingramcontent.com/pod-product-compliance
Lightning Source LLC
Chambersburg PA
CBHW031513210526
45464CB00007B/2896